Doctor

OM KIDZ
An imprint of Om Books International

In many cultures, it was believed that doctors were God's messengers because they had the ability to save human lives. Today, a doctor is also our friend.

All of us need a doctor at some point in time. Can you imagine what life would be like if there were no doctors to treat us?

The field of medicine is one of the noblest professions. Think about how many patients are admitted in a hospital every day. It is the doctor who treats and saves these patients!

Not only is the field of medicine a noble one, but doctors are received warmly wherever they go.

When a baby is born, it is the best moment for the parents. It is the doctor who makes sure that both the mother and the baby are fine.

Once you decide to be a doctor, there are many specialties that you can choose from.

Just like there are various organs in the human body, there are similar branches of medicine that focus on each organ.

A doctor handling a particular field is known as a specialist. So, you can be a dermatologist (skin), general physician (general health), paediatrician (children's doctor), cardiologist (heart doctor), dentist (teeth doctor), gastroenterologist (gastric system) and much more!

It is not easy to become a doctor, you need a lot of patience and have to study hard for it.

You have to get a degree, earn a license to practice and also complete a residency program. All this takes many years of hard work.

A doctor can never rest and must be very calm. The work is very demanding. Night or day, he or she is on call! For doctors, patients always come first!

A good doctor should always build a strong, and friendly relationship with his patients. He or she must also be a good listener and communicate clearly with his patients.

A doctor must be very organised and efficient. In this profession, there is no room for mistakes. One error can lead to serious effects, and some can even be fatal.

If being a doctor sounds like an exciting profession, you can gather more information about it from libraries and search engines online!